William S. Bush

The Liberal League and National Elections

William S. Bush

The Liberal League and National Elections

ISBN/EAN: 9783743321458

Manufactured in Europe, USA, Canada, Australia, Japa

Cover: Foto ©ninafisch / pixelio.de

Manufactured and distributed by brebook publishing software
(www.brebook.com)

William S. Bush

The Liberal League and National Elections

POLITICAL DEMANDS OF LIBERALS.

I.

PROPOSED POLICY.

It is proposed by some Liberals that the NATIONAL LIBERAL LEAGUE, without pledges from Hancock or the Democratic party, should unite and vote with that party. They insist that Hancock or Garfield will be elected : that no separate nominations be made, and that the League abandon its specific demands for this campaign, and take the democratic ticket on trust.

Liberals may be said to have definitely abandoned separate nominations in this campaign. Some will support Weaver. Others denounce him as a church member ; but that does not prove that he is a bigot. He is to-day battling for free speech, and an honest ballot in the Southern States. He defends the rights of labor. He stood up bravely in Congress against the despotic rulings of Speaker Randall, who with the applause of his party, centralized power in his own hands and throttled the right of petition and free inquiry. The Democratic Chairman of the Committee on Appropriations is an autocrat. The Democratic rank and file in Congress are afraid to do justice to honest claimants, fetter themselves with self-imposed rules, and waste the session in partisan investigations, and vigorous protests against presidential vetoes and bayonets at the polls, and in attempts to unseat honestly elected Greenback and Republican representatives so that they may have a majority of the States in case the people fail to elect a President.

The Greenbackers have fought the partisan schemes of the Democratic Congress, and have proved themselves in the South the allies of liberalism, in their demand for free speech and an honest ballot.

II.

DEMANDS OF LIBERALISM.

THE political demands of the Liberal League were declared in the resolutions of the Congress of 1879:

Resolved, That we deem it expedient for the Liberals of this country to act as a political organization for the accomplishment of the following objects:

1. TOTAL SEPARATION OF CHURCH AND STATE, to be secured under present laws and proper legislation, and finally to be guaranteed by amendment of the United States Constitution; including the equitable taxation of church property, secularization of the public schools, abrogation of Sabbatarian laws, abolition of chaplaincies, prohibition of public appropriations for religious purposes, and all other measures necessary to the same general end.

2. NATIONAL PROTECTION FOR NATIONAL CITIZENS in their equal political, civil, industrial, and religious rights, irrespective of race or sex; to be secured under present laws and proper legislation, and finally to be guaranteed by amendment of the United States Constitution, and afforded through the United States Courts.

3. UNIVERSAL EDUCATION THE BASIS OF UNIVERSAL SUFFRAGE IN THIS SECULAR REPUBLIC; to be secured under present laws and proper legislation, and finally to be guaranteed by amendment of the United States Constitution, requiring every State to maintain a thoroughly secularized public school system, and to permit no child within its limits to grow up without a good elementary education.

III.

THE NECESSITY FOR REFORM,

Is shown by the ostracism of infidels from office, from the witness box, and from social recognition in many of the Southern States, and by the vigorous denunciation of all independent voters. Free thought is branded as a crime, and independence as treason to the State. Tissue-ballots and fraud or force defeat the honest vote cast by the legal voters. Religious tests for office and for witnesses are exacted. An infidel may be robbed and his family murdered in his presence, in most of the Southern States, and he cannot be heard as a witness. To him the Courts are barred—justice is blind.

The principle of the old colonial codes, that Negroes and Indians might be enslaved because they were "Infidels"—that they had no rights Christians were bound to respect—that they could not be witnesses against Christian slaves—is still preserved in the exclusion of Infidels from office and from the witness stand. Within the year past Darwinians have been refused the right to testify in Maryland and Tennessee. The Negro, who is not an Infidel, is enfranchised; but in name only. He votes at his peril, except for the regular Democratic ticket, and election judges presume any other ballots to be void, and cast them out or count them on the other side.

In some of the Northern States, statutes and decisions made by Christian legislators and judges of the theocratic periods of the Colonies, still survive. Old Puritanic laws are enforced in a spasm of sanctity, or new laws enacted. Colonial statutes against blasphemy, enacted when it was a crime to think, when the church admitted only its own members to citizenship, when the town meetings were held in the meeting-houses and presided over by ministers, when Quaker women were publicly whipped naked from town to town in New England, and Unitarians were burned at the stake in England, are suffered to remain as land-marks of the barbarism of the early Christianity of this country.

The old Colonial dogma, that the church must be sustained at the common expense of the town, still exists in part in the form of voting public funds to sustain church institutions and charities, and in the exemption of church property from its equal share of the public taxes. The homes of the poor are taxed and sold for taxes to protect the untaxed palaces and property of the church.

Relics of barbarism still exist in many of the States:

In *Arkansas*, a person who denies the being of God, cannot hold any civil office in the State, nor be competent to testify as a witness in any court.

In *Delaware*, unbelievers are not allowed to testify.

In *Georgia*, *Indiana*, and *Maine*, religious belief goes to the credibility of the witness.

In *Maryland*, a witness is competent, provided he believes in the existence of God, and that under his dispensation, such person will be held morally accountable for his acts and be rewarded or punished therefor, either in this world, or the world to come.

No person can hold office who does not believe in the existence of God.

In *Mississippi*, the Constitution provides that no person who denies the existence of a Supreme Being, shall hold any office.

In *North Carolina*, it is provided that all persons who shall deny the being of Almighty God, shall be disqualified for office.

In *Pennsylvania*, in order to be a competent witness, " one must have his conscience alive to the conviction of accountability to a higher power than human law."

In *South Carolina*, a person who denies the existence of a Supreme Being, is not permitted to hold any office.

The Constitution of *Tennessee* provides, that no person who denies the being of a God or of a future state of rewards and punishment, shall hold any office in the civil department of the State.

Evolutionists are not competent as witnesses. Herbert Spencer or Darwin could not testify in any court.

Connecticut, *Delaware*, *Maine*, *Maryland*, *Massachusetts*, *New Hampshire*, *New Jersey*, *Pennsylvania*, *Rhode Island*, and *Vermont*, still maintain Statutes against blasphemy which were enacted in Colonial times by legislatures composed of church members, who copied the ecclesiastical common law of England.*

On suffrage the LIBERAL LEAGUE agrees with Benjamin Franklin, who stated the fundamental principles of government to be:

" That liberty or freedom consists in having an actual share in the appointment of those who frame the laws, and who are to be the guardians of every man's life, property, and peace; for the *all* of one man is as dear to him as the *all* of another; and the poor man has an equal right, but more need, to have representatives in the legislature than the rich one. That they who have no voice nor vote in the electing of representatives, do not enjoy liberty, but are absolutely *enslaved* to those who have votes, and to their representatives; for to be enslaved, is to have governors whom other men have set over us, and be subject to laws made by the representatives of others without having had representatives of our own to give consent in our behalf."

IV.

ALLEGED CRIMES OF THE REPUBLICAN PARTY.

The reasons assigned for abandoning the Republican party, are:

1. The postal laws, and conviction of Bennett.

2. Attempting to pass a "God in the Constitution" amendment.

---

* In France alone of self-governed countries, religious dissent is not a bar to political advancement. Still the enemy of progress there is the enemy of freedom here. Its leaders say :

" Religious liberty is merely endured until the opposite can be carried into effect."—*Bishop O'Connor*.

" If the catholics ever gain, which they surely will do, though at a distant day, an immense numerical superiority, religious freedom is at an end."—*Archbishop of St. Louis*.

" There is, ere long, to be a state religion in this country, and that state religion is to be Roman Catholic."—*Father Hecker*.

3. The Electoral Commission.
4. The National Election Laws.
5. Centralization of Power.
6. The nomination of James A. Garfield for President.

The first and second points are those relating particularly to the demands of the LEAGUE.

1. It is claimed that the postal laws declaring obscene matter to be unmailable, interfere with the freedom of the press, and are unconstitutional.

It is admitted that State Laws making it a crime to publish obscene books or prints, are constitutional. That State Courts, in enforcing them, may follow the rulings and decisions of the common law courts of England and of the Colonies. This is no crime against a free press. It is further insisted that the National Government has no power to "regulate" the mails, and it is therefore usurpation on the part of Congress to interfere with the sovereign police power of the States over the literature printed in the State, or imported into it.

On the conviction of Mr. Heywood in Massachusetts, T. B. Wakeman, Esq., addressed an indignation meeting in Boston, and said:

"You have long standing and sufficient laws on the whole subject in Massachusetts, and *if Mr. Heywood had been found guilty under them, I should have left the matter to you as her citizens; I should never have come here to enter a protest.*"

The precedents of the common law of England and of Massachusetts were followed in the United States Courts. The conviction of Carlisle in England in 1819, was for violation of the common law of England against blasphemous and obscene publications, by the publication of Paine's *Age of Reason.* The conviction of Kneeland in Massachusetts in 1834, was for publishing "a scandalous, blasphemous, and profane libel, in which he did wilfully blaspheme the Holy name of God," &c., saying, "Universalists believe in a God, which I do not; but believe that their God, with all his moral attributes, (aside from nature itself,) is nothing more than a mere chimera of their own imagination." On appeal to the Supreme Court, SHAW, J., in the opinion of the Court, said: "The indictment may be considered both as a charge of composing, printing, and publishing an impious, obscene, and blasphemous libel, and also as a direct charge of the crime of blasphemy." 20 Pick, 211.

The Attorney-General of the United States decided Heywood's book was not obscene, and President Hayes pardoned him. After that, D. M. Bennett was indicted, tried, and found guilty of mailing the same book, by a jury trying the case according to the rules of the common law and the decisions of State Courts.

The power given to establish post offices, has been held by Congress to include the power to regulate the mails, to define and punish postal crimes, and the statutes in 1810 and 1825 were so entitled. When Chief Justice Marshall was on the bench, no one questioned this power. Judge Field, in his opinion in the Jackson case, simply followed the early action of Congress and the prior rulings of the courts.

The Colonies had no postal system. The "royal mail" in the Colonies, was superseded by the Continental postal system of Congress in 1775, and has been purely a national matter from that day to this.

Justice Field says, in *Ex parte Jackson*, 7 Otto, 735:

"The validity of legislation prescribing what should be carried, and its right and form, and the charges to which it should be subjected, has never been questioned. * * *

"The power possessed by Congress embraces the regulation of the entire postal system of the Country. * *

"No law of Congress can place in the hands of officials connected with the Post Office service, any authority to invade the secrecy of letters and such sealed packages in the mail; and all regulations adopted as to mail matter

of this kind, must be in subordination to the great principle embodied in the Fourth Amendment of the Constitution.   Nor can any regulation be enforced against the
transportation of printed matter in the mail, which is open
to examination, so as to interfere in any manner with the
freedom of the press.

"In excluding various articles from the mail, the object
of Congress has not been to interfere with the freedom of
the press, or with any other rights of the people; but to
refuse its facilities for the distribution of matter deemed
injurious to the public morals."   7 Otto, p. p. 735, 736.

This was the unanimous opinion of the Supreme Court
of the United States, and disposes of the denunciation of
the law as unconstitutional because Congress has no power
to "regulate" the mails.

On the question of obscene literature, the LEAGUE

Resolved, That we are in favor of such postal laws as
will allow the free transportation through the mails of the
United States of all books, pamphlets, and papers,
irrespective of the religious, irreligious, political, and
scientific views they may contain, so that the literature of
science may be placed upon an equality with that of
superstition.

Resolved, That we are utterly opposed to the dissemination through the mails, or by any other means, of
obscene literature whether "inspired" or uninspired, and
hold in measureless contempt its authors, publishers, and
disseminators.

Resolved, That we call upon the Christian world to
expunge from the so-called sacred bible, every passage
that cannot be read without covering the cheek of modesty
with the blush of shame,* and until such passages are

---

* In 1833 Noah Webster published a revised edition of the Bible as a
"matter of moral duty," in which he altered passages by "the insertion
of euphemisms, words, and phrases which are not very offensive to
delicacy, in the place of such as cannot, with propriety, be uttered before
a promiscuous audience."   In 1842 he wrote of the common version,
that "many passages are expressed in language which decency forbids
to be repeated in families and in the pulpit."   His edition was endorsed
by the faculty of Yale College ; also by Methodist ministers who com-
mended it because the editor had "altered some words and passages,
which cannot be uttered before an audience without giving offence,
especially to females ; which words and phrases subject the Scriptures to
the scoffs of infidels."

expunged, we demand that the laws against the dissemination of obscene literature be impartially enforced.

General Garfield, in 1876, when a Democratic House was revising Secs. 3893 and 3894 Revised Statutes, called the Comstock laws, said:

"I wish to call his attention to a case I have been informed was recently decided in one of the courts in New York, in which the person was imprisoned in the penitentiary for a term of years, for being the publisher of a journal in which appeared a crazy contribution from George Francis Train, wholly theological in its character, in reference to the doctrine of the Trinity, in which not an obscene or scurrilous word was used at all. Although the judge stated, as I am informed, to the jury, that it could not be called obscene literature, nor scurrilous, yet it was blasphemous in the highest degree, and on that statement the jury found the publisher guilty, and he was sentenced to three years imprisonment. It has occurred to me, when the act we passed for a very proper purpose last year, is liable to constructions of this character, that we thereby enter the domain of theological opinion, bringing down upon men the *odium theologicum*—which is perhaps, worse than political odium, when passion is aroused—we ought to be exceedingly careful in all our legislation touching this subject.   *   *   *   *   *   *

"Where freedom of opinion and of the press lie on the border of obscenity is a difficult question to determine, and I, for one, would be glad if the Committee on the Post Office and Post Roads would consent to the reference of this bill to the Committee on the Judiciary, not because I have anything against my friend's amendment, but in order that they may go over the whole subject and inquire whether we have not used terms too broad and too general in the original bill, that no wrong may be done while we are trying to achieve the good which the bill was intended to accomplish."

Congressional Record, Special Session, 44th Congress, p. 696.

2. The God in the Constitution Amendment.

Such an Amendment was asked by certain citizens in a petition presented to Congress in 1874. It was referred to the Judiciary Committee, and an adverse report made by Benjamin F. Butler, which was adopted. Congress was then Republican.

In 1875, Hon. James G. Blaine, of Maine, offered in the House, the following Amendment:

ARTICLE XVI.

No State shall make any law respecting an establishment of religion or prohibiting the free exercise thereof; and no money, raised by taxation in any State for the support of public schools, or derived from any public fund therefor, nor any public lands devoted thereto, shall ever be under the control of any religious sect, nor shall any money so raised, or lands so devoted, be divided between religious sects or denominations.

It was referred to the Judiciary Committee, and reported back for passage, August 4, 1876. On the vote passing it, James A. Garfield, and every Republican present, voted aye. The Democratic vote was divided, Blackburn and Knott of Kentucky, and others, voting "no."

The Amendment was reported to the Senate, and there amended as follows:

ARTICLE XVI.

" No State shall make any law respecting an establishment of religion, or prohibiting the free exercise thereof; and no religious test shall ever be required as a qualification to any office or public trust under any State. No public property, and no public revenue of, nor any loan of credit by or under the authority of the United States, or any State, Territory, district, or municipal corporation, shall be appropriated to or made or used for the support of any school, educational or other institution under the control of any religious or anti-religious sect, organization, or denomination, or wherein the particular creed or tenets of any religious or anti-religious sect, organization, or denomination shall be taught. And no such particular creed or tenets shall be read or taught in any school or institution supported in whole or in part by such revenue or loan of credit; and no such appropriation or loan of credit shall be made to any religious or anti-religious sect, organization or denomination, or to promote its interests or tenets.   This article shall not be construed to prohibit the reading of the bible in any school or institution ; and it shall not have the effect to impair rights of property already vested.

SEC. 2. "Congress shall have power by appropriate legislation, to provide for the prevention and punishment of violations of this Article."

The clause in regard to the bible did not nullify the anti-sectarian portions of the proposed Article.   It did not compel the reading of the bible in the schools, nor permit it, but simply provided that this article should not be construed to prohibit its being read.   The Democratic senators opposed the Amendment as an interference with the sovereign rights of the States, and voted solidly against it.

These facts show that the Republican party was not in favor of "God-in-the-Constitution" Amendment.

The Republican platform of 1880, is as follows :

Fourth—The Constitution wisely forbids Congress to make any law respecting an establishment of religion, but it is idle to hope that the Nation can be protected against the influence of sectarianism while each State is exposed to its domination.   We therefore recommend that the Constitution be so amended as to lay the same prohibition upon the legislature of each State, and to forbid the appropriation of public funds to the support of sectarian schools.

The equal, steady, and complete enforcement of laws, and the protection of all our citizens in the enjoyment of all privileges and immunities guaranteed by the Constitution are the first duties of the Nation.

In General Garfield's letter of acceptance he says :

" I cordially endorse the principles set forth in the platform adopted by the Convention.   On nearly all the subjects of which it treats, my opinions are on record among the published proceedings of Congress. * * * But it is certain that the wounds of the war cannot be completely healed, and the spirit of brotherhood cannot fully pervade the whole country until every citizen, rich or poor, white or black, is secure in the free and equal enjoyment of every civil and political right guaranteed by the Constitution and the laws.   *   *   *   Whatever help the nation can justly afford should be generously given to aid the States in supporting common schools ; but it would be unjust to our people and dangerous to our institutions to apply any portion of the revenues of the Nation, or of the States, to the support of sectarian schools.   The separation of the Church and the State in everything relating to taxation should be absolute."

This fully satisfies the demands of Liberals as to taxation, and sectarian appropriations or religious tests for office.

The South has furnished the only successful " God-in-the-Constitution " movement.   It was headed by Thos. R. R. Cobb, of Georgia, a Presbyterian lawyer and defender of slavery.   He was successful in having the recognition of the Providence of God in the Permanent Constitution of the Confederate States, and by a tie vote only was defeated in his proposition to prohibit carrying the mails on Sunday.   He secured also the provision that no " law denying or impairing the right of property in Negro slaves shall be passed."

The Constitution of Arkansas, in 1836, provided that, "No person who denies the being of a God, shall hold any office in the civil department of this State, nor be allowed his oath in any Court."

The Constitution of 1866 had the same provision.   That of 1868, adopted under the reconstruction laws of Congress, prohibited religious tests for office, for voters, jurors, or witnesses.   The Democratic reconstruction constitution of 1874, enacted : "That no person who denies the being of a God shall hold any office in the civil departments of this State, *nor be competent to testify as a witness in any Court.*"

This rule of law governs trials of the common law in State and United States Courts in that State.

NATIONAL ELECTIONS.

I.

THE RESULTS OF THE WAR.

THE old dogma, born of despotism and fostered by the church, that citizens have no political rights, but only such franchises as the King, or Parliament, or Congress, or the State Legislatures, may confer, has been practically, prior to the war, the rule in this country. The Revolution was a protest against it. The Declaration of Independence denied its validity, and asserted the Rights of Man. The tory and church element combined to render the Declaration a dead letter. Constitutions and laws were construed in accordance with the precedents of judges educated in the theocratic doctrines of New England, or the ecclesiastical common-law of Great Britain. Voters were disfranchised, slavery protected, free speech made practically a crime, mob rule, at the demand of the South, used to suppress free speech at the North; and as the grand culmination of all, to bind the free labor of the North in bondage to Negro slavery, civil war was inaugurated.

The war not only struck down the chains of the black man, but emancipated the conscience of the North. In church and State a great advance was made toward absolute freedom of thought. The camp fire and battle field broadened the ideas of the brave men who composed our armies. They burst the manacles of custom and superstition. Freedom, justice, and reason, became the watch words of the defenders of the country. The inherent rights of manhood were revered as sacred. Having won the battle of freedom against slavery and secession, they demanded guarantees for freedom, that loyal men, black and white, should build anew Republican governments in the South.   They also demanded that the same guarantees of freedom, exacted by their fathers against the National government, should be exacted of the State governments. They demanded a definition of citizenship in the National Constitution, in opposition to the dogma that there were no citizens of the United States, but only citizens of States.   They demanded that the State should be prohibited from abridging the rights and privileges of citizens of the United States.   They abolished the clause of the Constitution which adopted the State qualifications for suffrage as a basis for national elections, and guaranteed to all male citizens of the United States of adult age and inhabitants of a State, the *right* to vote for Presidential electors, Congressmen, and legislative, executive, and judicial officers of the several States.   The right to disfranchise rebels or other felons was conceded on the principle that such men were enemies to the nation, who had as effectually forfeited their rights as though they had expatriated themselves.

II.

THE AMENDMENTS—THEIR MEANING.

THE Thirteenth Amendment struck down slavery.

The Fourteenth Amendment struck down State Rights, limited the legislative power of the States, defined and established national citizenship, recognized the right of suffrage as a right of American citizenship, and provided for its protection by the nation in both national and State elections. The right of a State to deprive a citizen of the United States, and resident of that State, of the right to vote for Presidential electors, and representatives in Congress, was denied, except as a punishment for treason or other crime.   The State had no longer power to disfranchise a citizen because he was colored, had not paid a poll tax, did not own personal or landed property, did not belong to a church, could not read a section of the constitution, was not a person of moral character, or had been so unfortunate, by the neglect or fraud of officers, as not to have his name on the roll of registered voters. The right of suffrage of male citizens was placed beyond the control of the State in all national elections. The sole privilege granted to the State was to disfranchise for sex or crime. But the organic law as framed and enacted by the representatives of the soldier freemen of the nation, did not stop here. As the executive, judicial, and legislative officers of the States were sworn to support the Constitution of the United States, the supreme law of the land, they placed the elections for such officers on the same basis as the election of Presidential electors and Congressmen. National qualifications for State elections were imposed, and Congress authorized to enforce and protect those rights. The States were still permitted to regulate the qualifications for local and municipal elections. State rights was thus cut up by the roots. The distinctive and cherished dogma of the Democratic party was annulled. The election of State officers was not only placed under the supervision of the nation, but the right of adult male citizens to vote for such officers was affirmed. This section not only denies the power of the State to take away from the people of a State the right to vote for executive officers, but requires all State judicial officers to be elected by the people. It struck down the centralization of power in the executive and legislatures of the States, and recognized the right of the people to vote for judicial officers. It was a protest of the people against the tory, church, and pro-slavery legislation by which they had been robbed of their rights, and State despotisms of the most infamous character, and centralization of power of the most despotic form, built up in the name of Republican forms of government. The foundation stone of slavery and secession—the sovereignty of the States—was swept away. The people of the United States put it under ban—relegated it to the grave of slavery and "the lost cause."

Nor was this all. Fearing that the States would disfranchise citizens at municipal and local elections, on account of race, color, or previous condition of servitude, the Fifteenth Amendment was adopted, which prohibited the abridgment of suffrage, on those accounts, at all elections. The exclusive and unlimited right of the State over municipal elections, was denied, and Congress empowered to enforce this Article.

III.

RECONSTRUCTION.

THE Thirteenth, Fourteenth, and Fifteenth Amendments were opposed by the rebel element of the South, and by the Bourbons of the North. The State governments of the rebel states had been abolished by secession. The State organizations in existence when the war ended, were part and parcel of the Confederacy, and expired with it. Not one of their officers was sworn to support the Constitution of the United States. No member of their legislatures had qualified by taking the constitutional oath. Their statutes, their acts, their judicial decisions, were not only illegal, but were enacted, executed, or rendered by men who had no more legal right to govern the loyal men of the South, than the generals who led the rebel armies. It was the right of force, not of law. A government of bayonets—not of the people. The loyal men of the South were governed by martial law, and not by *de facto* officers of the States. None of these officers had been elected at elections called by officers sworn to support the Constitution of the United States. The executive, legislative, and judicial officers of the South, claiming to be the state officers at the close of the war, were never elected or appointed in accordance with the forms of law, and never sworn into office under the constitution. Their credentials and commissions emanated, in fact, from the rebel camp—and their government rose with the bayonet, and fell with the rebel flag.

"A mere usurper in office can have no authority, and can perform no valid official act."—*McCrary on Elections.*

In *Pennywit, et al, vs. Foote, et al,* 27 Ohio St., 619, the Supreme Court of Ohio, held in regard to the Confederate State government of Arkansas:

"This usurping government was one unknown to the constitution, and in direct antagonism to it, and the authority of the federal laws and authority. It could acquire no legal authority over the people of the United States, and no actual power beyond the range of its guns."

The loyal men of the Nation, who had defeated these usurpers, refused to recognize their forms of government, as the legal State governments of the South. They demanded that the loyal people of the South, white and black,—the real States which had remained in the Union— should reconstruct their governments on the broad basis of equality of rights and government by the people. The lines were drawn. The Democracy demanded that the State officers, claiming to be the State governments of the rebel States, should be recognized as the civil power of those States, on the same footing as though there had been no rebellion. The negro was to have no political rights. He was to be free in name only. Their rebel state organizations were to be recognized as the state, and the army to be withdrawn, or to be subject to the civil power of such state officials. They demanded to be let alone, by Congress and the Nation. Vallandigham, Seymour, Tilden, and President Johnson, were ready to agree to this demand. They denounced Congressional reconstruction as unconstitutional. They opposed the Amendments as annulling the "constitution as it was."

IV.

HANCOCK'S RECORD.

GENERAL GRANT and a Republican Congress were opposed to them. General Hancock allied himself with the friends of the "lost cause," denounced Congressional reconstruction, issued order No. 40, and talked about the supremacy of the civil law, and the peace and quiet of the South. He was a candidate for President before the Democratic convention of 1868, and sustained the candidate and platform of that party. The element he served then, has now nominated him, and pledged to him the solid South. His letter of acceptance is devoted mainly to a statement of State rights dogmas, and expresses his devotion to the Constitution as it was, and the construction placed upon it by the Democratic fathers. It is evident that he accepts the Amendments—as his party accepts them—to be construed in accordance with the dogmas of State rights. He surrenders in advance to a Democratic Congress, if one is chosen, by his pledge to abide by its action. He has not a word to say on the separation of church and state. He demands that the polls shall be kept free from bayonets; but does not denounce carrying elections by fraud, nor demand the abolition of the poll-tax and registration laws of Delaware, Virginia, and other states, which deny the poor man the right to vote for Presidential electors and Congressmen at National elections.

"General Hancock represents the conservatism of the army, of family pride, we might almost say, of a privileged class."—*Richmond Despatch, (Dem.)*

He is the enemy of progress.

English is a merciless Shylock. The Democrats ask the people to support a "superb" aristocrat and a cormorant. They do not represent patient labor, honest industry, generous deeds, justice, equality, and manhood. They have no claims on the sons of toil—no claims on Freethinkers or Liberals.

V.

THE ELECTION LAWS.

THE cases of *United States vs. Cruikshank*, 2 Otto, 560, and *United States vs. Reese, et al*, 2 Otto, 214, admit the validity of the Fourteenth and Fifteenth Amendments. Justice Clifford, in his dissenting opinion in Cruikshank's case, admits that Congress has power to enforce the Fourteenth Amendment. At the last session of the Supreme Court the election laws were held to be valid. The right of Congress to enact the laws, and of the President to use the civil officers of the government to enforce them, cannot be questioned. It follows that the United States marshal, when he finds that he cannot by his marshal's posse, keep peace at the polls, may call upon the military arm of the government to aid him. In such case there may be bayonets at the polls, but the bayonets are there to aid the civil authorities to keep the peace, in subordination to the civil power. General Hancock needs to re-read his own orders. December 18, 1867, he issued an order:

"IX. Military interference with elections, unless it shall be necessary to keep the peace at the polls, is prohibited by law, and no soldiers will be allowed to appear at any polling place, unless as citizens of the State they are registered as voters, and then only for the purpose of voting; but the commanders of posts will be prepared to act promptly if the civil authorities fail to preserve peace."

If this means anything it concedes the right of the military officer commanding the troops at the posts to decide the emergency, and the extent of the force to be used at the polls. The crime of the Republican party, in the passage and enforcement of the Constitutional

Amendments, is, that it has restored the government to the position it rightfully held under the early decisions of the Supreme Court of the United States. Then the sovereignty was in the people as a nation. As a town had full control of purely local town matters, so the States had full control of local state matters. The nation, alone, was invested with sovereign rights. But those rights were not unlimited. The matter is well stated in the following cases :

"As a judge of this Court, I know, and can decide upon, the knowledge that the citizens of Georgia, when they acted upon the large scale of the Union, as a part of the 'people of the United States,' did not surrender the supreme or sovereign power to that State, but, as to the purposes of the Union, retained it to themselves. As to the purposes of the Union, therefore, Georgia is not a sovereign State. * * * * * * * * * *

"Even in almost every nation which has been denominated free, the State has assumed a supercilious pre-eminence above the people who have formed it. Hence the haughty notions of state independence, state sovereignty, and state supremacy. In despotic governments, the government has usurped, in a similar manner, both upon the State and the people. Hence all arbitrary doctrines and pretensions concerning the supreme, absolute, and incontrollable power of government. In each, man is degraded from the prime rank which he ought to hold in human affairs. * * * * * * * * * *

"Whoever considers, in a combined and comprehensive view, the general texture of the Constitution, will be satisfied that the people of the United States intended to form themselves into a nation for national purposes. They instituted, for such purposes, a national government complete in all its parts, with powers, legislative, executive, and judiciary; and in all those powers extending over the whole nation."

Opinion of WILSON, J., in *Chisholm, Ex., vs. Georgia,* 2 Dallas, 461, 466.

JAY, J., classed the sovereignty of the state, as the same with that of a city, and held that, " at the revolution, the sovereignty devolved upon the people, and they are truly the sovereigns of the country." *Ibid*, 472.

Judge Wilson, whose opinion has been quoted, was a member of the Pennsylvania Convention, which adopted the Constitution. His speeches in favor of the Constitution, not only carried it in his own State, but being published widely, were credited with having a powerful influence in other States. On the 11th of December, 1787, he said:

"It is objected to this system, that under it there is no sovereignty left in the State governments. I have had occasion to reply to this already, *but I should be glad to know at what period the State governments became possessed of the supreme power.* On the principle on which I found my arguments—*and that is the principle of this constitution—the supreme power resides in the people.*"

"The genius and character of the whole government seems to be, that its action is to be applied to all the external concerns of the nation, *and to those internal concerns which affect the States generally;* but not to those which are completely within a particular State, which do not affect other States, and with which it is not necessary to interfere for the purpose of executing some of the general powers of the government."

And in regard to the power to regulate commerce among the States, the Supreme Court held in the same case:

"This power, like all others vested in Congress, is complete in itself, may be exercised to its utmost extent, and acknowledges no limitations other than are prescribed in the Constitution." *Gibbons vs. Ogden*, 9 Wheaton, 195, 197.

Even Judge Taney, when not sustaining slavery, admitted that "the sovereignty of the United States, resides in the people of the various States," and refused to follow English precedents as inapplicable, holding "Our own Constitution and form of government must be our only guide." *Fleming vs. Page*, 9 How, 618.

GRIER, J., held: "The Constitution of the United States was made by and for the protection of the people of the United States." *League vs. De Young*, 11 How, 203.

"I do not admit that there is any *sovereign power*, in the literal meaning of the term, to be found anywhere in our system of government. * * * *Sovereign State* are cabalistic words, not understood by the disciple of liberty, who has been instructed in our constitutional schools. It is an appropriate phrase when applied to an absolute despotism. I firmly believe that the idea of sovereign power in the government of a republic, is incompatible with the existence and permanent foundation of civil liberty and the rights of property." *Gaines, et al, vs. Buford*, 1 Dana, Ky., 501.

VI.

THE ELECTORAL COMMISSION.

THE Democrats were not willing, in 1876, to have the electoral votes counted by the Vice-President of the United States. They had prepared a second set of returns from four States, from which they hoped to gain at least one elector. Under the rule that Congress had simply a ministerial duty to perform in footing up the votes upon the face of the returns, they expected to count in Cronin in Oregon, or the electors from Florida, South Carolina, or Louisiana. Legal and valid returns were made by the returning boards of the three Southern States. They devised the commission in such form that they expected a Democratic majority. The election of Judge Davis to the Senate ruled him out, and Judge Bradley was chosen as the fifth judge. His decisions in regard to the powers of the Commission, and in regard to which returns were regular, gave the requisite 185 votes to President Hayes, and he was declared elected. The Democrats chose their arbitrator and lost by seven to eight. Usually when parties agree to submit to the decision of a board, selected by mutual agreement, they are bound by it. There was but one mode of contesting the decision of the commission. Congress exhausted its jurisdiction when the vote was declared. The right of an appeal to the courts still existed, and the statute expressly reserved the right to open the question elsewhere. While the Democratic party has constantly claimed that Tilden was legally elected, no step has been taken to invoke the aid of the courts. Tilden accepted the finding of the commission and of Congress, that Hayes had 185 votes. His position as a political martyr, has been a source of consolation to his wounded ambition. Declining to be a candidate, his party lauded him as the legally-elected President, but defrauded of his office by the theft of the vote of *two* States. This is an admission that the Democratic claim in 1876, as to the electoral votes of Oregon, Florida, South Carolina, or Louisiana, was a fraudulent claim. No clue is given as to which two States of the four belonged to the Republicans. It will be time to answer the charge of theft when Hancock and English, who endorse the platform, specify the States referred to. The attempt to steal the electoral vote in Oregon never would have been made by the Tilden managers, if they had in fact been sure in law of one electoral vote from either of the other three contested States. The Electoral Commission held that Cronin had no right to vote as elector, and thus branded as fraudulent his electoral college.

The statute creating the Commission provided:

"SEC. 6. That nothing in this act shall be held to impair or affect any right now existing under the Constitution and laws to question, by proceeding in the judicial courts of the United States, the right or title of the person who shall be declared elected, or who shall claim to be President or Vice-President of the United States, if any such right exists."

If Tilden was lawfully elected President of the United States, he is entitled to the salary of the office. The

Court of Claims has jurisdiction of such suits. This law having provided for revision by the courts, if there was an error of law on the part of the Electoral Commission as to their powers, or if frauds had been committed in Louisiana, Florida, and South Carolina, that could have been proved in the Court of Claims. On the other hand, the incumbent of the office could have proved frauds in Alabama, Mississippi, and North Carolina—could have probed to the bottom the operations of Pelton, Smith Weed, Manton Marble, and Cronin—and the men for whom they acted. The fact that Tilden, with the approval of his party, did not seek a remedy in the courts, justifies the conclusion that the Democratic claim was baseless—that they knew Hayes was honestly elected, and if the honest vote cast had been honestly counted, Samuel J. Tilden would not have had 184 votes in the electoral college.

VII.

CENTRALIZATION OF POWER.

THIS charge is based on the allegation that the Republican party has usurped the power which should be exercised by the States, and infringes the sovereign rights of the States, in conferring power upon the United States marshals to appoint deputies for national elections, to make arrests for violation of the national election laws, and by providing for the appointment, by the courts, of supervisors of election. These officers are lawfully appointed; the power to appoint the officers and give them jurisdiction is granted in the Constitution. The supremacy of Congress over the elections for electors and representatives is conferred by the Constitution. The subject-matter is national. The people of each State have an interest in fair elections and an honest vote, and in a fair count. The Democratic party admit this in regard to elections at the North. They demand that the Fourteenth Amendment shall be enforced at the North. They have found in Rhode Island that a tax and property qualification for suffrage in the case of native citizens is exacted, as well as registration of such citizens, while in the case of naturalized citizens the ownership of $134 worth of land in addition is required. The Wallace committee investigated the case of Rhode Island, and the majority report affirms, "that the government of Rhode Island, under its present constitution, is nearer an oligarchy than a democracy;" * * that they are compelled "to recognize Rhode Island as different in her government, her institutions, and her policy, from all of her sister commonwealths in the Union, and lead us to grasp at any provision of the Federal Constitution which fairly construed, will grant us power to enforce for her people 'a republican form of government.'"

The committee having reached this conclusion, reported that Rhode Island has no right to a representation of two members of Congress if the proportion of disfranchised citizens is as great as they believed. Hence the committee reported a bill for an act to provide for such an enumeration of persons in the tenth census "as will clearly designate the basis of representation required to be made under the Fourteenth Amendment," and in their desire for a ballot free from bayonets, but not from fraud, they allowed the bill to be postponed. The committee knew not only that these state statutes were unjust, but that being in violation of the Fourteenth Amendment, they were void. The States were prohibited from abridging the right of adult male citizens from voting at national and State elections; and from abridging any privileges of citizens of the United States. The rule of law applies here as in the issue of bills of credit, or State bank paper.

c

In the case of *Craig vs. The State of Missouri*, 4 Pet., 436, Chief Justice Marshall held:

" It will not be questioned that an act forbidden by the Constitution of the United States, which is the supreme law, is against law," and utterly void.

" A State cannot do that which the Federal Constitution declares it shall not do." *Briscoe vs. Bank of the Commonwealth of Kentucky*, 11 Pet., 318.

In *Cohen vs. Virginia*, 6 Wheat, 414, the court held that " the Constitution and laws of a State, so far as they are repugnant to the Constitution of the United States, are absolutely void."

In *Cummings vs. State of Missouri*, 4 Wall, 322, the test oath clauses of the State Constitution, prohibiting persons from holding office or following the professions, unless they purged themselves of treasonable acts or sympathies, was held to be a bill of attainder, and void. This ruling was made in favor of those who sympathized with the " lost cause." Under the same rule, the poll-tax, property and religious disqualifications of voters and citizens in the Northern and Southern States, are bills of attainder subversive of civil rights, enforced by ministerial officers, without trial by jury, and are therefore absolutely void.

In Delaware, by an unfair apportionment, Newcastle County, with half the population of the State, has but one-third of the representation in the legislature. In 1878 thousands of voters were disfranchised because they had not paid a poll-tax. In 1880, to prevent the Republicans and Independents from gaining control of the State, the names of many more voters were stricken from the registration list, and the Democratic judges were compelled by the United States courts to reinstate them. It is conceded that the Amendments to the Constitution struck out the word " white " as a qualification for suffrage ; and by the same rule, the poll-tax qualification was abolished.

It has been decided, and rightly too, in Wisconsin, that an arbitrary registration law, which disqualifies every citizen otherwise entitled to vote, because he is not registered, is unconstitutional and void. The poll-tax and registration laws of Delaware are void; and the poor men and working men of that State should unite to overthrow the Democratic oligarchy which now plays the despot in the name of State Rights.

VIII.

THE REMEDY PROPOSED AND ABANDONED.

In accordance with these decisions, the committee should have reported that the State laws were nullities, that the restrictions were not binding on any citizen of adult age, and that their right to vote should be protected by supervisors of election appointed under the national election laws. In this mode, such illegally disfranchised citizens would have been protected, and their votes received and counted. Instead of meeting the question like men who were determined to enforce the law, and protect the constitutional rights of the native as well as foreign-born citizens, the committee proposed a measure which postponed all relief until after the next Presidential election, and the Democratic Senate dropped the bill itself. If the Democratic Senators had made the investigation in good faith, if they were determined to do justice, if they had made up their minds that a violation of the Fourteenth Amendment by State laws made such a government an oligarchy, and anti-republican, their report would have stated the law not as partisans, but as jurists. They would have investigated the case of other States whose Constitutions and laws disfranchise adult male citizens for other causes than treason or crime. In law, persons are held to have legal notice of whatever is shown by the record, whether they examine it or not. Hence these Democratic Senators knew that there were other States whose statutes violated the Fourteenth Amendment; that there were other oligarchies besides Rhode Island. That the State of Delaware enforced a registration and tax qualification which disfranchised thousands of her working men, that the people were not permitted to vote for judicial officers. They knew that the same state of facts existed in Virginia, disfranchising the poor white and colored men. They knew that the same class of laws were enforced in other States; that the election machinery of such States as Mississippi had been so arranged that the election officers were virtually appointed by the governor, and that the people were deprived of the right to elect the State judges who were to decide upon their rights under these laws.

Knowing this, the Democratic Senators knew that if their investigation extended to the Southern States, they would be compelled to report that the State organizations of Delaware, Virginia, Georgia, and South Carolina, were now oligarchies and not Republican forms of government. They knew that the "Home Rule" of Democratic rings in those States, was built up and maintained by the disfranchisement of the poorer class of citizens; and that if they did justice to all, they would strip the Democratic party of its majority in the House of Representatives, and place the control of the elections in the Southern States in the hands of Republicans and Greenbackers. To save their party they were blind to the facts except in Rhode Island and Massachusetts. To enable them, by the vote of the solid South in the electoral college, to elect a defender of State despotisms, they confined their researches for oligarchies to New England.

IX.

OLIGARCHIES DEFENDED.

HAVING nominated their ticket and professed to be in favor of a free ballot, their organ at the Capitol of the Nation states the facts, in part, in regard to Virginia. In the *Washington Post* of August 16th, under the head of "*Persecuted Black Republicans*," *The Post* says, that the Republicans were hilarious over the divisions in Virginia, but,

"It was discovered that the great mass of Virginia Radicals were as useless for political purposes, this year, as so many cows or coons, having been actually disfranchised by State legislation.

"But the intelligent public will understand that the statute by which a majority of the Virginia Republicans are disfranchised, this year, is in strict accordance with the Constitution as amended; that it applies to all classes, colors, parties and conditions; that its "cruel and relentless persecution" consists of a provision that no man shall vote who has not, on or before a given date, paid a poll tax of one dollar, and that, in order to prevent wholesale bribery and the voting of masses of ignorant men like cattle, it is made a penal offense for one man to pay this poll tax for another.

"That's the whole of it. The State of Virginia, through her law-making mechanism, says to every voter in the commonwealth that his right to the ballot shall be suspended during any and every year in which he may not care to pay one dollar for the exercise of the elective franchise. And is there a man of any party, in any section, who will stand up and say that such legislation is wrong? Ought suffrage to be made so cheap that a man who will not contribute one dollar a year to the support for local government shall have the same voting power as his honest, industrious, tax-paying neighbor? Does not the very fact that this act shuts a majority of the Virginia negroes out from the polls this year show that it is wise and timely?"

45,000 blacks, and 17,000 whites, the *Post* states, are disfranchised this year.

A year ago the reported disfranchisement of 71,000 voters would have taken away two representatives from that State. The fact remains that Virginia is an oligarchy according to the report of the Wallace Committee, and the right to make it so is openly justified. Virginia alone, of all the States, has made it a penal offense to pay the poll-tax or clerk's fees of a voter. No New England oligarchy has made poverty a crime to that extent.

The *Post* gleefully claims that the poll-tax law is constitutional because it does not violate the Fifteenth Amendment. That it violates the Fourteenth Amendment is conceded by the Wallace Committee of the Senate.

The Fourteenth Amendment prohibits the States from abridging the " privileges or immunities of citizens of the United States," in the first section, and in the second section, protects the right of suffrage as a right belonging to adult male citizens of the United States, inhabitants of a State. This is not to be construed in accordance with the old colonial rule that suffrage was a grant, a franchise to be given or taken away by the king.

The Fifteenth Amendment recognizes the right of citizens of the United States to vote, and prohibits the United States or the States from denying that right on account of color, race, or previous condition of servitude.* This Amendment applies to territorial and local elections,

---

* WHAT SOUTHERN SUPREMACY MEANS.

Congressman Blackburn, of Kentucky, in the House of Representatives, April 5, 1879.

For the first time in eighteen years the Democracy is back in power in both branches of Congress. We propose to celebrate her return to power by wiping from the statute book those degrading restrictions on freemen (the election laws), and by striking away the shackles which partisan legislation has imposed. We do not intend to stop until we have stricken the last vestige of your war measures from the statute book—until we have an untrammeled election and an unsupervised ballot.

as well as State and national elections. If, under these Amendments, a State may impose a penal poll-tax or property qualification, the United States may do the same. Any party making such an Act of Congress and disfranchising the working men of the nation, would be swept out of existence. State centralization is the only means by which the rights conferred by those Amendments can be annulled.

X.

THE NOMINATION OF GARFIELD.

THE crowning crime, charged upon the Republican party, is that their candidate for President is a Christian priest. General Garfield is eligible to membership in the League, and is entitled, so far as his priest-hood is concerned, to be its Presidential nominee. He is in favor of " the absolute secularization of the government," and complies with the sole test of the Cincinnati platform.

The Cincinnati Congress made the test simply "the absolute secularization of the government," and being " in favor of perfect civil and intellectual liberty." This is shown by the following resolutions :

Resolved, That we mutually pledge each other that we will, in our several localities, use our influence and cast our votes for such candidates for office as believe, and publicly declare their belief, in the absolute secularization of the Government, and we recommend that the State and auxiliary leagues in their respective localities act together upon all political questions.

Resolved, That we claim it to be the duty of every true Liberal to extend to all others every right that he claims for himself; that he cannot politically discriminate against any person on account of religious belief, provided only that such a person is in favor of perfect civil and intellectual liberty.

General Garfield is not a bigot. This is shown by his speech in Congress on the revision of the postal laws in 1876. He voted for the Blaine Amendment for the separation of church and State in 1876. He endorses the Republican platform of 1880, as shown by the emphatic statement in his letter of acceptance.

If Garfield has been a preacher in the church of the Disciples, he was such not by any ordination, pretense of apostolic succession, credentials from conference, synod, presbytery, or pope, but because in that denomination every man was his own priest. Every thinker was entitled to speak freely his own thoughts. Alexander Campbell, the founder of the Disciples church in this country, knew no ecclesiastical master. He was independent, and by his honesty to his own thought, his scholarship, his industry, he laid the foundations for much of the liberalism of the present day. If any proof is wanted, the Chicago Convention furnished it, when the West Virginians refused to pledge themselves to abide by the action of the Convention, and were bravely and successfully defended by General Garfield.

On the question of suffrage, he demands in national elections, "that every elector shall be permitted, freely and without intimidation, to cast his lawful ballot at such election and have it honestly counted, and that the potency of his vote shall not be destroyed by the fraudulent vote of any other person."

General Rosecrans, in a recent interview, states that while General Garfield was serving as his chief of staff, he was tendered the nomination for Congress in the Ashtabula district; that he hesitated about accepting it, and asked his advice. "I replied," says General Rosecrans, "that I not only thought he could accept it with honor, but that I deemed it to be his duty to do so. The war is not yet over, I said, nor will it be for some time to come. There will be many questions arising in Congress which require not alone statesmanlike treatment, but the advice of men having an acquaintance with military affairs will be needed; and for that and several other reasons which I named, he would, I believed, do equally as good service to his country in Congress as in the field."

Recurring to the nomination, General Rosecrans said : " I consider Garfield head and shoulders above any of the men named before the Convention, and far superior to any of the political managers upon the floor. He is a man with broad views, has always been a consistent Republican, and has a clean record. I cannot believe that James A. Garfield was ever guilty of a dishonest act. As the campaign progresses it will be found, if it is not now acknowledged, that Garfield is a hard man to beat."

With Garfield in the Presidential chair, we shall see needed reforms pushed forward, the right to the ballot and to a fair count sacredly protected, the rights of labor protected, a total separation of church and State, and broad and liberal views carried out in legislation, and in the executive departments of the government.

XI.

THE DEMAND OF THE HOUR.

LIBERALS should forego their private grievances, direct their energies to the establishment of and protection of the people in free thought, free speech, untrammeled and equal political privileges—to national protection of personal and political rights against violence, fraud and despotism under the forms of law. We must demand for others what we demand for ourselves. We cannot demand protection from the dogmas of priestcraft, and at the same time enforce the dogmas of kingcraft against the workingmen of the nation, black or white. We must demand that the rights of manhood shall be protected and enforced, by the strong arm of the nation, upon every foot of our soil. When such men as Blaine and Ingersoll, who concede the political demands of the Liberal League, stand by the Republican party and its candidates, we need not hesitate to join them in the grand work of establishing the national government on the broad groundwork of justice, equality, and protection to all citizens.

So long as the Liberal League stands by its platform of 1879, its members can have no alliance with the Democratic party—the party that clings to the dead past, and year by year brings out in their filmy shrouds the ghosts of "State Rights" and "the Constitution as it was," and honors them as living realities.

The Liberal League cannot take a step backward. It cannot join the party that lives in the memory of its coward statesmen and its judges who revered the decisions and dogmas of royal judges and worshipped as sacred the antiquated edicts of titled robbers. It must still place the rights of man above the rights of state or national organizations, and demand for all citizens, without respect of race or sex, the same rights which its members claim for themselves as the rights inherent to manhood.

The Democratic party has made the issue that it has a right to disfranchise whom it pleases, that the colored man and the poor man have no right to vote, and the infidel no right to hold office, unless they choose to permit it. It is the party of prejudice, intolerance, barbarity, and fraud. Tissue-ballots, the shot-gun, business and social ostracism, and counting out the honest vote, and counting in candidates whether elected or not, are its chosen means of success. The contest is but another form of the same forces which upheld slavery. It is no longer a race contest. It is not directed against the African alone. It is not sectional. The intent of the Democratic aristocracy is to prevent the poorer classes, black and white, especially the laboring men of the country, from having any voice in or control of the government. If successful, the centralization of power in the State governors of the South will be increased, so that free thought and independence of action will be crushed out. There can be no progress. Liberal views will not be tolerated. The statutes which deny justice will not be repealed. The rule of the Christian aristocracy will be firmly established; new religious tests instituted: the old colonial doctrine, that none but Christians have political or personal rights which governments are bound to protect and respect, will again be the statute rule of the States which claim a sovereign right to legislate on the subjects of religion and suffrage as they please, so that the legislation is not based on discriminations of color.

No Liberal who is true to the principles of free thought, free speech, a free and honest ballot, the sacredness of individual rights over the rights of the corporations known as State governments, can for a moment think of voting for Hancock. The Democratic party is the party of pretense and promise, of cant, centralization, and crime, of force and fraud, of ostracism and outrage, of political slavery and partisan sovereignty. With it, the party is the State, treason to the party, treason to the State—the President and Congress the agents of the State officers, and the courts of the United States official boards to register the decrees of State courts.

No honest Greenbacker who believes in the rights of labor and the sovereignty of man, can ally himself or vote with such a party. No Republican with the memories of the past before him, in justice to the heroic dead and the living victims of partisan hate and oppression, can desert GARFIELD AND ARTHUR.